RUFUS

by

Karl Pruter

🌐
BORGO PRESS / WILDSIDE PRESS

www.wildsidepress.com

RUFUS

by

Karl Pruter

St. Willibrord Press
Higlandville, Missouri
1994

copyright
Karl Pruter
1994

CONTENTS

WE WON'T BRING HOME THE FIRST
DOG WE SEE...................... 1

CHILDREN....................... 5

RUFUS DISCOVERS SILVER DOLLAR
CITY 9

TOYS 18

RUFUS AND NANCY 23

THE MANY FRIENDS OF RUFUS 27

TRAVEL AND BOARDING KENNELS .. 34

HOOTEN TOWN -- THE DAY WE
NEARLY LOST RUFUS 39

THEOLOGICAL LESSONS LEARNED
FROM RUFUS 41

WE WON'T BRING HOME THE FIRST DOG WE SEE

Our house had been without a dog for about six months and we missed having one. My wife and I decided to go to the Animal Shelter, just to look and see what they had available. We told each other that we were not going necessarily to bring home a dog and positively we would not bring home the first dog we saw.

We had never before met a "Rufus". When we arrived at the shelter there was a row of large cages and the first dog that caught our attention was a big red dog that looked like an Irish Setter. He was sitting there with a forlorn look which he obviously had practiced for the benefit of any visitors that might come along to adopt a dog. He studied us and our car but otherwise appeared only to enjoy his misery.

We went in and talked to the good people that ran the shelter and told them that we wanted to look at any dogs that were available for adoption. They took us inside the building which ran along the back side of the cages we had seen outside. About a dozen dogs were inside of various sizes, shapes, colors and breeds. When we came there was a commotion and the big red dog came to see what was going on. Of all the dogs he seemed most happy to see us and indicated it not only by wagging his tail, but his entire and very immense back side. I did look at a Dalmation, who looked at me, and indicated that he could take me or leave me. The red dog was anything but indifferent and since we had been told we could walk any of the dogs we asked one of the employees if we could walk the "setter". She came with a collar and opened the cage and attempted to place it on the dog. It was much too small and she said she had to go back to the office for a larger one. As soon as she closed the cage door, the dog let out loud barks of protest, and kept it up until she returned with a collar which was twenty-four inches and which she was able to put on him. With that, the dog quieted and quickly started for the way out. He seemed so pleased with us that we decided, "Yes, we will adopt him." After the paper work was completed we started to go out, led by this big dog who knew exactly which car was ours and which subsequently became his.

As soon as I opened the back door of the car, the dog was in. He placed his rear on the back seat and stuck his head between the two bucket seats occupied by my wife and myself. Fearing, he might get car sick, my wife, Nancy, gave him a lot of attention. We soon found out that he never got car sick or tired of riding in the car.

On the way home we discussed the fact that on his cage at the shelter there was a sign that read, "Outside dog". My wife said, "I don't want an outside dog. What is the point of having a dog if he doesn't come inside with you." I suggested to her that the sign might have been there because the shelter operators figured most people would not take such a big dog unless they thought they could keep him outside. She then admired his red color and said, "I think Rufus would be a good name for him. He looks like a 'Rufus'". The dog apparently thought so too because he quickly responded to the name. Who knows, he might have already had that name, because it surely fits.

When we arrived home we parked the car in the drive and as soon as we let Rufus out he headed for the front door and waited to be let in. "I guess he has been in a house before," Nancy remarked. Very quickly we got the impression that Rufus had probably never spent a night out of doors. He quickly surveyed the house and decided it would do. It also became apparent to us that he was well trained. He never got on the furniture. That is, before we got him. He didn't do it afterwards either until he discovered friends of ours who succumbed to his manipulative ways. But that's another story.

When we went out into the yard, Rufus explored every corner and apparently discovered two significant scents. Obviously, he knew we had a dog before we got him but he was nowhere to be seen. The previous dog had a pal named, Sheba and she had been in the yard often. When he finally met Sheba he instantly accepted her as a friend, although he has never made friends with any other dog. He considers all dogs as potential rivals for his owners' affection, and he will greet them with a certain reserve, but if his owners attempt to pet another dog that brings an end to his tolerance. Rufus then trots out his mean, "I want to eat you alive, bark." We never petted Sheba, not wanting to end his friendship with her. Every dog should have, at least, one friend among his own kind.

However, Rufus seems content to be a "people" dog. He likes people. All kinds of people. But he has two special types of which he is especially fond. Big men are tops. And they seem to like him. I can't recall how many have come up to Rufus tousled his ears, and look at their wives and said, "I want to get me a big old red dog like this." And he likes children. Oh boy, does he like children.

CHILDREN

We have always thought that Rufus came to us from a home where there were children. He loves children. As far as he is concerned children have three sterling attributes which adults do not have. First, they will with almost no exceptions, like to pet dogs. Second, if they have cookies or other edible items in their hands, if you are quick, you can steal them. Third, it is a cinch to lick the faces of babies in strollers. New mothers get upset, but mothers with several children are glad for the help in keeping little faces clean.

About the exceptions. Rufus with his hundred and twenty pounds seems enormous to very small children, and they get frightened at the mere sight of him. This creates problems when older brothers or sisters have already accepted Rufus as a special friend. One day while walking with Rufus a nine year old boy sitting in his mother's parked car invited Rufus to come join him. No sooner was Rufus in the car and screams of anguish emanated from the rear of the vehicle. A four year old brother was terrified by the beast that had come into the little car. His mother came out of the hair salon to see what the commotion was about and as she looked in the car she said, "It's only Rufus" and urged him to come out. I apologized and she replied, "I suspect, Billy, invited him in." Months later the younger boy got to know Rufus and joined the ranks of his many admirers.

When we go to Silver Dollar City children come by the score to pet Rufus. The more cautious ones sometimes ask, "Does he bite?" and I reply, "No, but he swallows." To most children this is a funny reply but every now and then some child jumps back quickly and gives me a quizzical look. Usually other children laugh at him, and he quickly joins the ranks of those petting Rufus.

One reason for Rufus' popularity is that a half dozen children can easily pet him at the same time. There is enough dog to go around. At the part, many adults are intrigued by this and take photos of Rufus surrounded by a half dozen or more children. When he lies down very young children are tempted to crawl over him, and on him. He has never been know to object even when they twist his nose, or his lips. To him children can do no wrong.

Some times they come into the yard and engage in rough play which Rufus likes, but as you can imagine when it happens a lot of children get knocked down. Rufus never jumps on people but he leans against them and when he turns quickly, whoever is in the way had better have a secure footing, or be as heavy as Rufus. In fact, they had better be heavier.

Rufus is a smart dog, and his definition of children is flexible. He doesn't go entirely by age and size. We had a number of volunteer workers from a local day care center for the mentally handicapped. When they came Rufus greeted them with his usual enthusiasm. They were older people and big people, but Rufus obviously discovered their mental handicap and decided they were children. That meant to Rufus that they would play with him, and they did. He also knows that when children have cookies you can steal the cookies with impunity. Sure enough at lunch time, he soon had one man's sandwich. The man was upset, but not because he lost the sandwich but from the ravenous way in which Rufus devoured it he concluded that poor Rufus was hungry. In fact, he said, "The dog is starving! Look at him eat that sandwich!" Of course Rufus wanted to consume it all before I or some adult caught him and took it away from him. The next time the handicapped folk came they were careful, having learned about Rufus' stealing ways. But like children, they all fed him part of their lunch. Not even adults escape the pathos behind his big, brown, starring eyes.

Children really like Rufus. I could tell many stories but one of my favorites happened when we still took Rufus to a boarding kennel when we went on trips. This particular kennel raised Shelties and had about forty dogs. When we returned from our trip, a day early, we expected that Rufus would be waiting for us in the kennel. The owner's house was next to the kennel, and in the yard was Rufus playing with the owner's three children.

They didn't explain why they were playing with Rufus, when they had forty dogs of their own. They didn't need to, after all, if you can play with Rufus, why play with just any dog?

RUFUS DISCOVERS SILVER DOLLAR CITY

When April comes to the Ozarks, my wife and I, always purchase a season pass and visit Silver Dollar City. The City is a theme park, built around the handicrafts of the 1890's. They have barrel makers, glass blowers, blacksmiths, basket makers and just about every handicraft you can think of. You can watch a man make a chair and then, if you wish, buy it.

The City also features a lot of entertainment. They have music groups, both indoors and out of doors. At the gazebo, just after you come in, they feature the Horse Creek Band, which plays country music, The River Rats, who play New Orleans Music and the Cajun Connection which is pure Cajun.

One day shortly after Rufus came to live with us we discovered that you were allowed to bring a pet with you. Since Rufus was unhappy whenever we drove off and left him we decided to see how he would do at Silver Dollar City. If Rufus had ever dreamed of a Doggy Heaven he obviously had Silver Dollar City in mind. No sooner had we arrived we realized Rufus was a hit with many people. Not only children, but many adults came and wanted to pet Rufus. Before the day was over, at least, a hundred people, came up and asked if it was all right to pet the dog. They made a wide range of remarks, but two were repeated over and over again. "He is a beautiful dog!" and "Boy, he sure is a big un!" Not a few women remarked that his hair is absolutely gorgeous! During our many trips to Silver Dollar City we met many men who upon coming up to Rufus to pet him would turn to their wives and remark, "Some day, I'm going to get me a big old dog like this." Some of the wives seemed less than pleased but most of them smiled in amusement. It wasn't any surprise to us that Rufus enjoyed the people and the fuss they made over him.

The big surprise was his reaction to the various bands. I can't remember which one he heard first, but, I think it was the Horse Creek Band. We found a seat on a bench and Rufus sat in the aisle. When the first number was over and everyone applauded, Rufus barked. When the applause stopped, he stopped. Everyone was surprised and half the audience laughed. During the second number people apparently were wondering what Rufus would do when the number was over. They were not disappointed, when they applauded Rufus barked. During the entire performance Rufus gave his approval along with the audience.

The first day with Rufus we listened to three bands and he reacted the same way for all of them. I also learned that he would not bark if I petted him. At one number the audience liked the performance, and began to applaud while the band was still playing. I never do that, and since I was petting Rufus I continued petting him, and he did not join the applause with his barks. So, Rufus quickly learned when he could bark and when I did not want him to. The beauty about this way of controlling the dog, was that it was not easy to detect. But more about that later.

Whenever we came to Silver Dollar City, we brought Rufus. He is more fun than anything we do, see or hear! One of the best times we had was during the International Show. It was early in the season and Silver Dollar City brought musical groups from many nations. One group Rufus liked was Bulgarian. He seemed to like the beat of the music and would enthusiastically bark for each and every number. There was a couple behind us and after one number, the man turned to his wife and said, "That was a good number but I don't think it was a five woofer."
The Rumanian group were very pleased with Rufus and sang one song in English for him. They changed the words of a familiar American song, just a trifle. You would recognize it. It began like this, "How much is that doggy in the audience?" Rufus really gave a "four woofer" for that one.

Knowing that the visiting groups were guests in this country and not used to some of the informality of our entertainment, we were concerned that Rufus not offend any of them by his antics. We had heard that Turks were not especially fond of dogs and were very pleased when many of them came after their show to pet Rufus.

One man, who spoke no English, pointed to his teeth and then to Rufus and looked at us with a question on his face. I shook my head, "No", and he quickly came and petted the dog. A German group asked me, in German, "Does he bite?" and I replied in German with my line, "No, but he swallows." The man thought it was so funny he repeated it in German and didn't seem to notice that the audience did not understand the language. We have often wondered if some of the visitors from Germany, Bavaria, Estonia, Latvia, Ireland, Italy, Switzerland, Rumania, Bulgaria and France told people back home in Europe about the American dog who liked their music so well, that he barked after each and every number.

As far as Rufus is concerned his favorite group remains the Cajun Connection. The beat of the music is one he seems to enjoy and then he likes to watch Terryl and Kelli do the Cajun dances. Terryl is also a comedian and he and Rufus became great pals. At first, Terryl would come up to me and asked who I was and where I was from. He would then asked the question, "Does your dog bite?" The audience always enjoyed the response, "No, but he swallows" and my wife quickly tired of hearing it. Terryl also would take a rubber alligator which was about eighteen inches long, and show it to the audience and tell how Cajuns would prepare alligator for dinner. He would add, "You know, Cajuns will eat anything." While he walked about showing the alligator, Rufus would watch with great interest. Occasionally, when Terryl was almost finished with his spiel, I would let Rufus off his leash. Like a flash the audience would see him come out from nowhere and grab the alligator from Terryl and bring it back to me. Terryl would come down and make a feeble attempt to take it from Rufus, but he never trusted Rufus enough to attempt to pry open his jaws. He could have and after a pro-forma struggle Rufus would have surrendered it. I always had to retrieve it for Terryl.

The nice thing about Rufus' visits to the City is that he learns new things. We had visited the park for over nine years when he tried something quite new. Danny Eagan, a hillbilly performer sang a song one day about a dog. Instead of words for the chorus, he substituted barks and I let Rufus join in. He matched Danny, bark for bark. I don't know whether Danny or the audience was more thrilled. Now not every performer would want to do a duo with a dog. But Danny comes from a suburb of Booger Holler, Arkansas and he would tell you, himself that his Mamma brought him up not to be too proud to join up with another singer even though he might have four legs and a tail.

But, maybe my readers think I am a mite too proud of my dog and maybe even think I exaggerate about his talents. So, let me give you the Rufus' story as told by my friend, Archbishop Donald Mullan. He came with us to Silver Dollar City and was impressed enough by Rufus to write the following account for the St. Luke Magazine.

RUFUS STEALS THE SHOW

SEEING IS BELIEVING

You had to be there to believe it. And I was there. Wife Cathy and I were visiting Bishop Karl Pruter in Highlandville MO - site of the world famous Cathedral Church of the Prince of Peace. World famous because it is listed in the "Guinness Book of World Records" as the world's smallest cathedral seating only 15 people. Services are held three times daily.

But the Cathedral isn't Bishop Pruter's only claim to fame. He is not only a recognized author of Christian books and literature sold world-wide he also is the proud owner of a nine year-old 120 pound dog named Rufus. And Rufus is what this column is all about.

DOG IN A MILLION

Rufus is no ordinary dog. Part Irish Setter and part St. Bernard Rufus can only be described as friendly. Somebody drops by or even comes close and Rufus is there tale awagging and awaiting some of that lovey-dovy petting stuff.

But Rufus is more than that. He is a celebrity. Bishop Pruter told us that Rufus accompanies him on visits to the nearby Silver Dollar City Country Music Theme Park about 20 miles away.

That Rufus is allowed in.

Greeted fondly by almost everyone -- park staff calling him by name.

And even allowed to enter buildings where major stage shows are held.

Rufus, in turn, sits quietly beside the bishop during a performance. And when the audience breaks into applause, if he likes the particular performance, Rufus barks.

Performers not only thank the audience, but single out Rufus.

We accompanied the two to Silver Dollar City for opening day celebration of their Old Time Country Christmas featuring one hundred miles of lights.

We were to see for ourselves just what kind of celebrity Rufus really is.

IT DIDN'T TAKE LONG

We had just arrived at one of several mammoth parking lots and were walking to the tram that takes you to the city, when somebody hollered out, "Hi Rufus!"

And when the tram arrived, Rufus took his seat with the rest of the noon-hour crowd, only to be welcomed and introduced to everyone by the PA announcer who gave instructions during the trip.

Of course, the tram staff had to pet Rufus before takeoff, treating him like a long-lost friend.

Arriving at the entrance gates to the city, it was the same thing all over again.

And once inside, many visitors had to inquire about the dog, pet him, and give him treats. (No wonder Rufus likes going to Silver Dollar City.)

One elderly lady wasn't so friendly.

"Imagine bringing an animal like that here," she said to her friend, shying away from Rufus but making sure we could hear.

Bishop Pruter explained to us that the reason Rufus is so welcome by the park staff is because he is well behaved and doesn't do his business anywhere inside the park. Rufus, in an afternoon-evening visit, bore that out.

AND THEN, THE UNEXPECTED

We entered one of the many outdoor areas where country singers entertain and took seats in the front row. The show opened with greetings to all for turning out on such a cold day with a special word of welcome to Rufus.

And all through the day, every few minutes, somebody would shout, "Hello, Rufus."

Christmas at Our House, featuring the David Peel family was our first inside show and as expected, Rufus would bark at the most appropriate times, much to the delight of the audience. But the Peels, knowing the big, red-haired canine, took it all in stride with special mention along the way.

Highlight of the day was the indoor presentation, "A Cajun Christmas," featuring Cedric Benoit and the Cajun Connection and Redneckers." And Rufus, unexpectedly, had a starring role.

ALL PART OF THE ACT?

Keith Allen, who turned out to be one of the star singers in the show, was warming up the crowd with a quasi clown act. He wore a set of cloth antlers to look like a reindeer and ever so often would take them off and put them on somebody in the rapidly filling auditorium.

Just before the curtain went up, he walked along the front row shaking hands - his antlers in the other hand. When he reached us, Rufus grabbed part of the antlers, Keith didn't let go and knowing the good-natured dog and being a veteran entertainer, he engaged Rufus in a tug of war. Spotlights shined upon the pair as the audience ate it up. It ended in a draw, the antlers king, Keith retaining half, Rufus the other. Both got a big round of applause and the incident was mentioned several times during the show. Many of the people thought Rufus was all part of the act and that he was at every show.

Wonder what the negative lady thought if she had been present?

Regardless, Silver Dollar City is worth the trip south. And if you go, time it with a Rufus tour or visit the famous dog at the world's smallest cathedral.

(written by Bishop Donald M. Mullan and published in the St. Luke Magazine, Niagara Falls, Canada.)

TOYS

I don't know where or how Rufus got his first toy, but one day Rufus came home with me from the post office and when we got in the yard he had a small teddy bear in his mouth. Obviously he had picked it up in someone's yard on the way home. Which child in the neighborhood had his teddy bear stolen I had no way of knowing.

Rufus brought the bear into the house and whenever anyone came to the door he would run and get the bear and show it to them. He would come to them and make growling sounds. When they tried to take it from him he would draw away. He wasn't offering to them, he was showing it to them. It was his toy.

The second toy he acquired was a gift. Two men, Tom and Cobb, had a shop where they manufactured cedar furniture. We would visit them and Rufus would run around the shop looking for a block of wood or a stick that he could show them. One day, he discovered a stuffed rabbit about ten inches high. After that he would always look for the rabbit and show it to everyone who happened to be in the shop. He did this quite often and finally Tom and Cobb told him he could keep the rabbit. Once he had it home he would alternate with the teddy bear. When someone came to the door he would grab whichever one of the toys was handiest and proudly show his prize to whoever came for a visit.

On one of his visits to Silver Dollar City, he acquired another toy. We were watching the Cajun Connection Show and Rufus finally gave Cedric, the leader of the band, three woofs after one of his numbers. Cedric told the audience, "After seven years, Rufus, finally gave me three woofs." When we left Cedric gave him a ten inch rubber alligator. Rufus proudly walked out of the theater with the alligator much to the amusement of the crowd that left with him. Now when people come to the door, at home, he picks up his alligator to show them and insists that they notice. If they don't he paces the floor of the living room growling and crying until they pay attention. After all he earned this toy.

But Rufus has been given some very common place things to play with that he likes as well as his toys. Men's caps have always interested him. One time when I took him to the James River for a swim two men swimming in the river began to toss a cap between them and Rufus swam back and forth trying to get the cap. And he did too. I don't know who had the most fun that day, Rufus, the swimmers or those of us who stood on the river bank cheering for Rufus. One of the regular visitors to our house, is Eddie Davis and he has a red stocking cap that caught Rufus' eye. When Eddie would come in he would attempt to put his cap in a shopping bag which he always carries and Rufus would attempt to grab it. When he failed he would stick his nose in the shopping bag and help himself. Some friends of ours decided to make sure Rufus had a cap of his own so they bought Eddie Davis a new one and he in turn gave his to Rufus. The same friends also gave Rufus a pair of gloves as it seemed Rufus had an equal love of gloves as for hats. Was Rufus happy?

Well, yes, but now that he had a glut of toys, Rufus lay down one evening with his rabbit and proceeded to chew it up. There didn't seem to be any reason for it. He just wanted to chew it up. So you see, you can't always figure out dogs. Rufus, had his teddy bear for eight years, and it is still in fairly good condition. But then dogs do eat rabbits, but few are able to tackle a bear.

RUFUS FOR LIFE

Picketing is not my cup of tea. I had never done it, but when I learned that one million six hundred thousand babies a year, were being killed in abortion clinics each year in the United States, I decided I needed to voice my protest. Springfield, Missouri used to have two abortion clinics but one was finally closed, and I would like to think that Rufus and I were partially responsible.

Every Monday Rufus and I would go to the Springfield clinic and march up and down the sidewalk in front of the clinic. I carried the sign in one hand and held Rufus' leash in the other. The sign on one side had a picture of a baby with the slogan, "Love and Protect Babies" and on the other it simply said, "Rufus says, 'My mother was a bitch, but she gave me birth.'"

Rufus was really a great help. A lot of people are antagonistic towards any kind of picket, but a man with a dog can't be all bad. As a matter of fact, I am certain many people who might have been hostile smiled upon seeing the dog, and paid attention to the message. Also, I would most often be the only picket and I figured if the people inside would kill a baby for two hundred dollars, what might they do to someone who cost them a few clients? Rufus while not a hostile dog was big enough to be intimidating.

One day when we were picketing we were joined by another picket from a town west of Springfield. He and his group tended to be very confrontational in their approach and soon he and the landlord of the building had an argument. They shouted at one another and Rufus began barking at the landlord. The landlord became very angry and shouted at me that he did not want my dog barking at him. I told him very quietly that if he did not shout Rufus would not bark. He lowered his voice and Rufus just watched him silently. We picketed many times after that and the landlord was always very pleasant and <u>always</u> spoke in soft tones.

Most people were very pleased to see us there. As they drove by in their cars they would wave and as they got to know Rufus, they would call out to him by name. In fact, I can honestly say the people were enthusiastic because I kept count of their responses. In their enthusiasm many responded with a thumbs up sign. A few got carried away and put up the wrong finger, but I figured it was half of a victory sign.

There were a few that were truly aggressive and threw pop bottles, but fortunately for Rufus and I they were terrible shots. Others, on the other hand on hot days brought soda for me and water for Rufus. Usually, someone stopped to thank us personally, saying, "I can't be here, but I am glad you are, thank you." Those words meant a lot to both of us.

RUFUS AND NANCY

Rufus likes me, he respects me and he obeys me, but it was my wife, Nancy he really loved. She was the one who named him, and the one who usually fed him. Also we both served him the same dog food, but when Nancy did it she usually added people food to it.

Nancy suffered from a number of ailments including Parkinsons and sleep apnea. She tended to fall a lot and shortly after Rufus came to us she fell over him and hurt herself rather severely. The doctor advised getting rid of Rufus, but we talked it over and decided Rufus should stay. But I did tell my wife that Rufus was rather large and if she fell, she should not fall over him, but on him. It did happen a number of times and Rufus never minded, but after her fall on him, he would come and lick her hand as she got off of him and tried to get to her feet.

Unfortunately, Nancy's sleep apnea began to take its toll and she soon suffered from dementia and became very confused. Her doctors met (she had six) and put her under medication which exacerbated her falling. Rufus came to the rescue. In that period she fell ten times and Rufus managed to anticipate it and get between her and the floor or ground, and she never was injured. In the ten times, he succeeded in nine and once had to race across the room to get to her before she fell.

The doctors figured Rufus couldn't always succeed so they took her off the medicine and she improved physically. The medicine hadn't helped her mentally either and the dementia continued to get worse. She would go up and down the street looking for her mother. Her mother had died many years ago and, if she had lived, would have been one hundred and seven years old. I would point this out to her but she was adamant and would often go out and make this futile search.

She would also get in the car, with Rufus, waiting for me to take her home. I would tell her that she lived here with me and Rufus, but she would argue and say she didn't live here. Often I would get in the car and go to the grocery store or take a ride and when we returned to our house everything would be all right. Sometimes she would get in the car and then get out to do something or walk down the street and forget poor Rufus.

Since I checked on her often, I would notice Rufus in the car and let him out. At one period I found Rufus in the car almost everytime I went out. I was puzzled until our neighbor, Helen Meyers called me on the phone one day and said, "Rufus is in the car and I wonder if you know what is going on?" I pleaded ignorance and she explained that Nancy was going down the street, looking for her mother and Rufus decided that it was not a good idea. When Nancy would start to leave the yard, Rufus would put his huge bulk (120 pounds) between her and the road and not let her get by. He frustrated her continually in her attempts to leave the yard, when she hit upon a scheme. She would go to the car and call Rufus, and, of course, he would jump in expecting to be taken for a ride. Then Nancy would close the door and go traipsing down the street. Well, Rufus soon figured that one out and instead of blocking her way he went with her to see that she came to no harm.

Although Rufus was Nancy's constant companion she always said he was my dog. At night when we sat in the living room to read or watch TV, Rufus was always near me. If I left the room he would go to Nancy, but come to me as soon as I would return.

At night he slept on the floor at the foot of our bed. He would stay there but if he heard thunder he would get up quickly and sit by Nancy's side of the bed. Somehow he felt safer with her during those times than with me. There were times when he was definitely her dog.

When Rufus was nine years old, Nancy died in her sleep one day. The paramedics were called and after a futile attempt to revive her they pronounced her dead. They then called for the coroner and asked if someone could get Rufus out of the room. Helen Meyer said, "I'll get him, he will come for me." Any other time, maybe but this time he wanted to stay with his mistress and he lay down beside her. Nobody attempted to remove him. She was his mistress and it was time for him to mourn!

THE MANY FRIENDS OF RUFUS

Losing Nancy was hard for myself and for Rufus. I had been married to her for forty-nine years and Rufus knew her for all but two years of his life. We were very fortunate in having a lot of friends who came to our support. Rufus, of course, has many more friends and acquaintances than I do. At Silver Dollar City hundreds of people know him by name. They haven't any idea who I am, except some of them remember me as the man who comes with Rufus. People in Springfield who drive by the abortion clinic when both of us are there sometimes meet me elsewhere and they do recognize me. What they say to me is, "Oh, I remember you; you are the priest who pickets the abortion clinic with Rufus." I can't even figure out how they have learned his name, but I know they don't know mine.

Of course, we have a lot of friends in common. Our closest friends are Dale and Phyllis Miller. When Nancy died it was Dale, whom I called at his place of work and he came to help me through that most difficult day. Dale and Phylllis are siblings who live with their parents and a half dozen dogs and as many cats. They like Rufus and he likes them. As far as I know, he has not been a bad influence on them, but they are a bad influence on Rufus. Let me give you an example. When Rufus came to our house, we discovered he had been carefully trained not to go on the furniture. He never did, and that was, before Dale and Phyllis. They usually came and Rufus would show them his toy and they would sit on the couch and make a fuss over him and admire his toy. Naturally, I was pleased that he liked my friends and they liked him. But one day I came into the room and there was Rufus sitting between Dale and Phyllis and looking very very pleased. I scolded Rufus and he got off. But when the Millers come he tries to convince them to let him sit on the couch again, and they tell him that he is trying to get them in trouble again. Although he has never been allowed to repeat his indiscretion, the Millers are, I am sure, his favorite people.

The lady who lives across the street from me, must be next on his list of favorite people. Helen Myer has dogs, cats, ducks, geese, and chickens in her yard, all living together in relative peace. I have asked Helen from time to time how many dogs or cats she has and she is never quite sure. Of course, Rufus can see she likes animals, and therefore a person to be trusted and admired. Whenever he sees her in her yard feeding the beasts he greets her with furious barks. Sometimes she comes over to see him and if he is in the yard, he hurriedly looks for a stick to show to her. Like with his toys, he doesn't let her have his offering but he wants her to notice and admire it. All day long

Rufus keeps track of Helen's movements. He seems to know when she is in the yard and asks to go out so that he can watch her. If she comes close to the fence, or goes to her car he greets her with his barking. And when she comes over to see him he is in ecstasy.

Of course, Rufus doesn't give anyone but his master, and perhaps the Millers, unconditional love. Helen offended him one day when she asked us to take her to the packing house to get bones for her dogs. She came out of the packing house with a big box of bones and placed them on the back seat of the car. Now Rufus is not allowed to have bones, because he always gets sick whenever he eats one. He didn't bother the bones on the back seat because he knew he wasn't allowed to have any. But when we arrived at Helen's house, she took the bones out and went into her yard and gave them to her dogs. Rufus was so outraged that when I drove into our yard and let him out, he immediately, ran to Helen's gate and barked in protest. Helen realized her faux pas, went into her house and cut some meat off the bones, cooked it and brought it out to Rufus. The next time we went to the packing house Rufus expected to receive his share when we returned, and although Helen refrained from feeding the dogs while he could see her, he immediately went to the gate and barked. Helen was amused, said he was a smart dog and got him some chicken which she had in her refrigerator.

As the best of friends are wont to do, Helen one day decided to tease Rufus. She had just taken her car out of her yard and was closing the gate and noticed Rufus at the end of his driveway barking to get her attention. So, after closing the gate, she walked over to pet Rufus and then said to him, "Rufus, you are so nice, I think I will steal you and take you home with me." Rufus reacted immediately, stopped barking and lay down on the ground. He wasn't going anywhere with anyone, including his very special friend, Helen. Helen is convinced Rufus understands almost everything people say to him. That day, she felt she had proof positive.

Rufus has lots of friends. There is Eddie. Didn't Eddie let him take his hat? There are Cobb and Tom, who gave him the bunny, and Jim and Peggy, who make a fuss over him whenever they come. (He does draw the line at staying with them when I go on a trip.) Larry Sloan, who owns The DeSales Catholic Bookstore is another very special friend. Whenever, I go into the store, Larry insists that I bring Rufus in so that he and his assistant, Vickie can pet him and introduce him to the customers. When, Larry first met Rufus he referred to me as Rufus' daddy. I like Rufus but I am his friend and most definitely not his father. But, a lot of people label a dog's master, "daddy". So I figured, if I am the dog's "daddy" and Larry and I are brothers in Christ, Larry must be Rufus' uncle. I am sure one reason why Rufus is so welcome is that he is always well behaved. Well, almost always. He did discover in the store, on a shelf near the floor, votive candles. He took one one day, and discovered they were very tasty and before anyone noticed started to eat a second one. So when I bring him in, I do have to steer him past the candle section. I wish Uncle Larry well, but I don't want to become one of his major candle customers.

Rufus has many, many, friends and I can't include them all, but I do not want to close this chapter until I tell about one more. Most people see Rufus and it is love on first sight. He is their friend and they are his. But once in a while, he has to use all his canine wiles in order to win a new friend. Some people do not like dogs and never will, but others who only think they don't like dogs can be won over. My number two son was one of these.

When Bob was growing up we almost always had a dog and/or a cat in the house. Bob played with whatever animal lived with us and seemed to like them all. (except a dog we called, the Bird but that is another story) In due time Bob left the nest married a very wonderful woman, named Margaret. She is a perfect wife for Bob, but she does have a major character flaw. She does not like animals, birds and reptiles and has convinced Bob he doesn't like them either. When we visited Bob and Margaret's home we always left Rufus back home in the Ozarks, but we did bring him on one trip. Bob looked startled when we drove up, and I quickly assured him that Rufus would sleep in the car. It was no problem for Rufus because the van was an extension of his home. After we were there for a while Bob suggested that we might like to let Rufus come in the fenced back yard. Rufus felt at home there, although when night came we let him go into the van to sleep.

The following day, Nancy and I wanted to go downtown and again Bob suggested we let Rufus stay in the yard. We agreed. When we returned Bob was in a lounge chair reading a book. Next to him sat Rufus and you know who had his arm around his neck and was petting him. Another day, when we left, Bob suggested we leave his leash, so that he could take Rufus for a walk. Rufus took it all in. When we returned Bob told us with considerable enthusiasm. "You know that dog is smart! He not only knew he was going to be taken for a walk, but he knew who was going to take him. He kept looking at me until I got his leash and we went down to the trace for a walk. When we came back, he didn't want to come into the yard. I guess, he thought it wasn't enough of a walk. So I took him around two blocks and then he was satisfied." We thought it was neat, not only that Bob enjoyed taking Rufus for a walk, but that Rufus was able to convince him to make the walk just a bit longer.

No, the story doesn't have a perfect ending. Bob has not gotten a dog. However, on his next visit to the Ozarks he did pet Rufus and he took him for a walk. He is making progress.
Margaret? Well, she hasn't joined Rufus' many admirers. She can't you know. Margaret has never heard the birds sing. She says, "They twitter". Of course, Rufus doesn't twitter. Danny Eagan would tell her, "Rufus sings."

TRAVEL AND BOARDING KENNELS

Nancy and I were always active in many things. The Church, several businesses and the fact that our children were widely scattered made it necessary for us to travel a great deal. Now that Rufus had become a member of the family there seemed to be a problem. At first we tried placing him in boarding kennels. One was called Happy Hollow and on the few occasions that we took him there everything seemed to go well. The people were nice, the kennels were clean and when we came to get him he was groomed and smelled of doggy cologne. But with each trip he showed more and more reluctance to go in to the kennels. Coward that I am, I would leave when they pulled and pushed in an effort to move 120 pounds of canine resistance.

I tried a second kennel and, the first few times went all right. But one day, I brought him there and when I handed the leash to the kennel owner Rufus lay down on the floor and cried. When I went out to the car and told Nancy she said, "I'm sure, that is why I didn't go in with you." What to do?

I thought I had a solution when I thought of Jim and Peggy Henry. They attended our church and whenever they came, Rufus was extremely pleased to see them. They raised dogs and so had kennels and when I approached them

-34-

they said they would be delighted to take care of him. The first few times went well. Rufus didn't spend all of his time in the kennel. He went around with Jim and even watched him while he repaired his cars and trucks.
But one day when we had to take a trip we brought Rufus to the Henrys. Knowing that he was going to be left again, Rufus refused to come out of the van. It took the three of us to lift him, take him out and place him in the kennel. That was the last time we boarded Rufus.

We take him wherever we go and it is a pleasure. We found that Knight's Inn and Motel 6 will take small pets. Of course, one manager in Illinois did point out to me that their directory said, "small pets" and she didn't think Rufus came under that classification. I argued, successfully, that it probably applied to all dogs and cats. In any event Rufus wasn't a problem then, and never has abused his motel privilege. Only twice has he been refused.

Again, our pleasure was increased by having Rufus with us on our travels. He frequently sat up front between the seats and stared out of the front window. When he got tired he would lie down between the seats or get up on the seat behind us and lie down. Of course, he took up the whole seat. When we had other people with us he share **his** seat reluctantly. Sometimes our passengers, knowing how Rufus felt about it, would sit on the seat directly behind him.

Rufus almost never wants to stick his head out of the window, like many dogs. However, when I turn off the highway, onto a secondary road that goes through a wooded area, Rufus insists on having his window open. I guess, the forest offers new and interest scents. My son, Bob, says he is just overwhelmed by all the trees he could mark if he were allowed to run among them.

Another time when Rufus wants to have his head out of the window is when we come to a drive-up window of any kind. At the local bank he knows when I get my deposit receipt there will be a dog bone for him. There is only one bank drive-up window in town where they do that but Rufus persists in trying at each and every one. He protests when nothing is forthcoming, but his plaintive barks go unheeded.

One day on a trip to Oklahoma City he surprised us. He is always curious about what takes place at the toll booth. Perhaps he is looking for biscuits or perhaps he is just interested. But he is usually a silent observer. This day, however, was different. We were just getting off the turnpike where the toll was two dollars. I gave the attendant a ten dollar bill and he quickly handed me change. Rufus immediately began to bark furiously and angrily. I looked at my change and noticed I had only received three dollars and called it to the attention of the attendant.

Whereupon, he apologized and gave me the rest of my change. What is remarkable was that Rufus began to protest before I counted my change. How he picked up on the fact that something was wrong with the transaction, I do not know. Further, each time we have taken that trip, if we encounter the same attendant, Rufus voices his displeasure. Yet, no harsh wordshad passed between the attendant and me. But Rufus knows.....

   Perhaps, most remarkable about Rufus travels is their length and duration. He has gone with me to California and on that trip we traveled nearly five thousand miles. We also make frequent trips to Canada and New Mexico. Everywhere we go people are intent on spoiling him. In Niagara Falls, Canada we visit the Cathedral of St. Luke. They insist he come into the offices and from time to time they feed him. I don't know and don't want to know what and how much they give him.

   Because of my position in the Church news has gotten around concerning Rufus and the fact that he travels with me. Whenever I stop somewhere, someone is sure to ask if Rufus is with me and express an interest in meeting him. By now, dear Reader, you know how fast he makes new friends.

   One time my son, Stephen, came for a visit and expressed an interest in going to Silver Dollar City. For some reason he asked me not to take Rufus with us. So I left him home in the house. It turned out to be a most visit. As we boarded the tram, the driver wanted to know, "Where is Rufus?" The man who took our tickets wanted to know. People stopped us constantly as we walked through the park, wanting to know, "Where is Rufus?" It was embarrassing to both Stephen and me.

Of course, the performers were concerned and finally I thought of the perfect answer. "Where is Rufus", one of the Cajuns asked. So I told him. "Rufus is in Springfield. He decided to see the movie, 'Beethovan ll'". It may not have been a good answer but I stuck with it for the rest of the day.

Now do you understand why it is almost impossible to go anywhere without Rufus? I just had a terrible thought. If Rufus went to Silver Dollar City without me, people would stop him and ask, "Rufus, where is what's his name?"

HOOTEN TOWN
THE DAY WE NEARLY LOST RUFUS

    If you live in the Ozarks you can travel to towns with such colorful names as Booger Holler, Yellen, and Hooten Town. Hooten Town is about seven miles from home and is on the James River. Rufus and I go there often in the summer because Rufus likes to swim. It is his favorite swimming hole. I usually throw a stick for him to get and he brings it back to me innumerable times. When he gets tired of the game, instead of giving me the stick, he takes up and drops it in front of the van.
    When it is really hot, I take Rufus to Hooten Town two or three times a week. Consequently, he regards it as his territory and won't tolerate any other dogs there. I came down one day and there were all ready two dogs playing along the river bank. Rather than risk a confrontation, I continue to drive to another place up river where Rufus often swam. The water was a bit high and at this point of the river, the water was quite swift. I didn't worry because Rufus is a very powerful swimmer. I threw the stick out to the middle of the river and Rufus swam out and grabbed it. Just then the current caught him and swept him down river to where a fallen tree lay across three quarters of the river. There was a great deal of brush against it and when Rufus hit it, he turn and started to swim back up stream when

once more the current swept against the branches. This time he slipped through and disappeared. I raced along the shore but when I passed the tree and the branches, Rufus was no longer in sight. I followed the river for about a quarter of a mile and saw nothing of my dog. I was convinced that when I threw the stick into the water I had sealed his fate.

   I gave up the search and returned to where he had gone into the river. A woman was sun bathing and I asked her if she had seen him, and she said, "Yes, after you left he swam around playing with his stick." Just then Rufus came up behind me and nuzzled my hand. He seemed glad to have found me! But not nearly as glad I was glad to see him. I never took him back to that place on the river. We stuck strictly to Hooten Town.

THEOLOGICAL LESSONS LEARNED FROM RUFUS

   Have patience with me Reader, I am not going to tell you that Rufus is a theologian. Remarkable as he is and while he may be smarter than most theologians, he is just a simple dog and is unlearned, never having been admitted into a theological seminary. But I learned some important lessons from him, nevertheless.
   A well known vet once said "My dog thinks I am the most wonderful, the the most powerful, the most intelligent, and the kindest being in the world. and I am not about to ask for a second opinion."
   Dogs are like that. Rufus loves me. He wants not only to be with me, all of the time, but he wants to please me. He applauds the musicians at Silver Dollar City by his barks, not just because it is fun, but because he knows it pleases me. He is obedient. I mean obedient! He likes to chase cats and when they come into his yard he is after them in a flash. But cats are smart, and the neighborhood cats know that once they reach the end of our driveway and are in the street, Rufus will stop. His master doesn't allow him to leave the yard. It is really sad to see Rufus racing madly to catch the cat and then brace all four legs and stop because he knows I do not want him to leave the yard. It occurred to me that to Rufus, I am his Master but more than that I am his god. You are probably god to

your dog also. It sounds flattering and it is. But then we are apt to say, "He is only a dog." Ponder that for a minute. Do we always want to be with God? Do we always want to please God? Does he have our absolute love, attention, and fidelity? In short, our dogs are better behaved, and more faithful to their gods, than we are to our God.

No matter how you view it. No matter how you try to explain it, the dogs come out ahead. I suspect a lot of people don't like dogs because of their very intense devotion to their masters. i.e. gods. It makes the unfaithful, the unloving, the ungrateful and those who are indifferent to their God, feel guilty and uncomfortable.

People often look down upon dogs because they will often continue to give unconditional love to a master who beats and abuses them. We, on the other hand, are asked to love the Creator who has given us life, and showers us with nothing but His Blessings.

Obviously dogs are noble creatures. Forgive me if I say that Rufus is the most noble of them all.

www.ingramcontent.com/pod-product-compliance
Lightning Source LLC
Chambersburg PA
CBHW051718040426
42446CB00008B/956